BREAKING OPEN *the* SCRIPTURES

Inspiration and Professional Growth

IMPRIMATUR

☩   Most Reverend
    Robert J. McManus, STD,
    Bishop of Worcester,
    June 26, 2017

Twenty-Third Publications
1 Montauk Avenue, Suite 200, New London, CT 06320
(860) 437-3012 » (800) 321-0411 » www.twentythirdpublications.com

Cover photo: ©iStockphoto.com / FangXiaNuo

ISBN: 978-1-62785-289-0
Library of Congress Catalog Card Number: 2017941591
Printed in the U.S.A.

CONTENTS

INTRODUCTION

The theme of this book responds to the call of Pope Benedict XVI and the bishops at the October 2008 worldwide synod: "The Word of God in the Life and Mission of the Church." The synod highlighted the importance of Scripture formation as fundamental to the faith life of today's Christians. This call is central to our ministry as catechists.

It has been fifty years since the publication of the *Dogmatic Constitution on Divine Revelation* (*Dei Verbum*, DV), one of the sixteen documents of the Second Vatican Council. This document is mentioned several times in this book. It would be wonderful if every catechist read the document, which is very brief—only twenty-two articles divided among six chapters. The phrase *Dei Verbum*, Latin for "Word of God," is taken from the first line of the constitution. (This is a common practice for Church documents.)

The *Dogmatic Constitution on Divine Revelation* outlines the many ways God has spoken to us throughout salvation history, summarizes how Divine Revelation is transmitted from generation to generation, discusses the interpretation of Scripture and the purpose and meaning of the Old and New Testaments, emphasizes the importance of Scripture in the life of the Church, and encourages us all to read and pray with God's word.

In the seven chapters of this book we are invited to study and pray the word of God as individuals and challenged to find creative and authentic ways of leading our students to the Bible.

1

The WORD of GOD: RELEVANT and POWERFUL

MARGARET RALPH

Scripture is just one of many expressions of and meanings for the word of God. In this chapter, we will first explore five meanings of the phrase "the word of God." Then, based on this broader understanding, we will discuss just why the word of God is so relevant and powerful in our lives.

The Meanings of the "Word of God"

If there were no Word of God, nothing would exist, including us. This is true because two meanings for the Word of God are: (1) the pre-existent Word that existed before anything else existed, and (2) the creative Word through which everything else that exists came into being.

We read about the pre-existent Word of God in John's gospel: "In the beginning was the Word, and the Word was with God, and the Word was God" (John 1:1). John then goes on to say about this pre-existent Word: "All things came to be through him, and without him nothing came to be" (John 1:3). This creative Word of God is described in Genesis 1:1—2:4. In this story, God's creative word is spoken at the beginning of each of the six days of creation. What God speaks becomes a reality: "God said: Let there be light, and there was light" (Genesis 1:3). "God said, Let there be a dome in the middle of the water…And so it happened" (Genesis 1:6–7).

Still a third meaning for the Word of God is Jesus himself. John goes on to tell us that "…the Word became flesh and made his dwelling among us…" (John 1:14). Jesus is the pre-existent Word of God who became flesh and dwelt among us.

Two additional meanings for the Word of God refer to two of the ways in which the Word of God continues to dwell among us. These are Scripture and Tradition. Through Scripture, God reveals to us what we need to know for our salvation. Through Tradition, the Church echoes those truths that God has revealed to each succeeding generation.

Scripture and Tradition have a totally interdependent relationship. Were it not for Tradition there would be no Scripture. It is the people of God, both Jews and Christians, who, filled with the Spirit, decided which books would be included in Scripture, that is, which books would be considered canonical and which ones would not. At the same time, the Church (the people of God) is not above Scripture but is ruled by Scripture.

What does "the Word of God" mean? Among its meanings are: the pre-existent Word, the creative Word, Jesus Christ, Scripture, and Tradition. As we will see, there is nothing in our lives more relevant or more powerful than the Word of God.

The Relevance of the Word of God

We have already observed that if there were no Word of God nothing would exist. Nevertheless, just for the sake of discussion, let us affirm the first two meanings of the Word of God, but not the other three. What would our lives be like if the Word had not become flesh, if there were no Scripture, and if there were no Tradition? As we probe the answers to these questions we will discover the profound relevance of the Word of God in our lives.

Jesus, the Word of God, is the fullness of God's self-revelation to God's people. Because the Word of God became flesh and dwelt among us, we know that God is love; that God loves every single person; that love, not legalistic obedience to law, is what God asks of us; and that we are not slaves to sin—we have been redeemed.

As catechists we will want to thank God every day for becoming flesh and dwelling among us. Had the Word of God not become flesh we would not be able to teach the truths that we almost take for granted. How do we know that what we teach is true? Because our source for those truths is the Word of God, Jesus Christ.

What if there were no Scripture? If there were no Scripture, Jesus' contemporaries could have received the revelation that he offered but subsequent generations would not have been able to receive the same gift.

Of course, much of Scripture—what we now call the Old Testament—took form before the Word became flesh and dwelt among us. It is not that the existence, the presence, or the power of our Trinitarian God became a reality with God's incarnation in Jesus Christ. It is that the human race was able to comprehend these truths through the revelation of Jesus Christ.

As catechists—echoing the Word of God through every generation—we must be lifelong students of the Bible. Remember, "the entire Christian religion should be nourished and ruled by sacred Scripture" (*Dogmatic Constitution on Divine Revelation*, n. 21), not by just the New Testament, not by just those parts of the Bible that appear in the Lectionary. How can we be faithful catechists unless we have read and studied the entire Bible?

What if there were no Tradition? Through Church Tradition the truths that Jesus made known to the human race, and to which Scripture gives witness, are faithfully passed on and applied to new contexts for every generation. It is the responsibility of the Church, through the guidance of the Holy Spirit, to interpret Scripture and to apply the truths taught in Scripture to these new social settings.

Through Tradition the Church teaches and guides every generation to live in fidelity to Jesus Christ and the gospel in very different social settings. As catechists, we pass on this Tradition with authority. We do not teach simply to pass on our own understanding of things, but to pass on the truths revealed by the Word of God through Jesus Christ, through Scripture, and through Church Tradition. What could be more relevant to the well-being of our world, our local communities, our families, and ourselves than echoing the Word of God with fidelity?

Both Scripture and Tradition Are All-Important

If we had Scripture and not Tradition—that is, no authoritative voice to interpret Scripture—Scripture would be open to constant misinterpretation. History has taught us this lesson, and we do not want to repeat the errors of the past. An example will make this point clear.

During the United States Civil War, well-meaning Christians supported the social institution of slavery by quoting the Bible: "Slaves, be obedient to your human masters with fear and trembling" (Ephesians 6:5). Can we, as Christians of the twenty-first century, use this passage to support slavery?

We cannot. The Church has spoken with authority on the way we are to interpret Scripture. (This topic will be addressed at length in a future article in this series.) It is part of Church Tradition that we interpret every scriptural passage in the context in which it appears in the Bible. We must consider the literary form, the beliefs of the time of the original author and audience, and the fact that Scripture presents us with a 2,000-year process of coming to knowledge in order to determine the intent of the original inspired author. Only then can we put the authority of Scripture behind our conclusions.

The Power of the Word of God

It is one thing to "know." It is another thing entirely to have the power to do something about that which we "know." Through the Word of God, through Jesus Christ, we have the *knowledge* of how to live so as to please God. We also have the *power* to do so. We name this power in various ways. Sometimes we call this power the "Holy Spirit." Sometimes we call it "grace." No matter what we call this power, the effect is the same: We are able to talk the talk *and* walk the walk.

How does the Word of God have power in our lives? There are many ways, but we will discuss four of them. The Word of God has power in our lives because of its authority, because Scripture is a living word that can be a light unto our paths, because the Word of God nourishes us in Eucharist, and because the Word of God sends us on mission.

Because of its authority: Christians are to be ruled by Scripture. Why do we give this one expression of the Word of God such authority in our lives? Because we believe that, in one sense, God is the author of Scripture and that through Scripture God has chosen to teach us the truths that we need to know for our salvation.

When you think about it, this is an amazing claim. Why should we, limited as we are, believe that we know how to live so as to please God? What makes us think that we understand the moral order? What gives us the conviction that our lives have purpose and meaning? Why do we hope and believe that there is life after death? The answer to all of these questions is that we believe that the Word of God—God's self-communication through Jesus Christ and through Scripture—has taught us these things with authority.

Because Scripture is a living word: In addition to teaching eternal truths with authority, Scripture is a living word. That is, it can speak to each of us individually about the most personal and private aspects of our lives. It can teach us how to walk in Christ's ways.

It is because we believe Scripture is a living word that we proclaim it in liturgical settings. We want to invite those in the community to experience the power of this living word in their own lives. It is because we believe Scripture is a living word that we teach catechumens and candidates how to *break open the word*. We are inviting them to hear this living word in conversation with their own inmost thoughts.

It is because we believe Scripture is a living word that we incorporate it into prayer services, use it as the basis for faith-sharing groups, and make it central to all of our catechetical lessons. Scripture, as a living word, can empower change in each of us individually, in our communities, in our whole world.

Because the Word of God nourishes us in Eucharist: We are not only to be ruled and guided by the living word, we are to be nourished by the word. How does the Word of God nourish us? In addition to giving us Scripture as a living word, the Word of God nourishes us through Eucharist. Remember that one of the meanings for the Word of God is Jesus Christ. Jesus continues to become flesh and dwell among us through Eucharist.

> Jesus continues to become flesh and dwell among us through Eucharist.

Through Jesus we not only have a companion on the road (companion means "one with whom we break bread"), but this companion, Christ, nourishes us. We receive the word into ourselves, and we become what we receive: the body of Christ. Just as physical nourishment empowers our physical bodies, so does this spiritual nourishment empower us to live out the gospel of Jesus Christ.

Because the Word of God sends us on mission: At the end of our Eucharistic celebrations, the celebrant often dismisses us with the words, "Go and announce the Gospel of the Lord." We are sent on mission. What is our mission? In John's gospel, Jesus explains the mission with these words: "I give you a new commandment: love one another. As I have loved you, so you also should love one another" (John 13:34).

Those who live out this mission raise families, serve the poor, work for justice, and try to transform the world through the power of the Word of God that dwells within them. They also become catechists.

Your Thoughts

1 How do I experience the Word of God in Scripture and Tradition? How do I nurture these experiences daily? Be specific.

____

____

2 What would my life be like if the Word had not become flesh, if there were no Scripture, and if there were no Tradition?

____

____

Try This

- Review the five descriptions of the phrase "the Word of God" and order them in terms of their importance and experience in your life. Consider how your understanding of this phrase impacts your faith, your teaching, and your lifestyle.

- Consider a current social issue that is impacting your community. What factors do you need to consider to fully understand the depth and breadth of the situation? How might your understanding of Scripture and Tradition enable you to reflect upon, interpret, and respond to social issues?

2

The WORD of GOD as GIFT

MOST REVEREND ANTHONY BOSCO

*That we are made in God's image is not because of our body. If we accept the astonishing statement that we are like God, we must realize that the similarity is not in our frail physical body but in our immortal soul, our psyche, our **anima**.*

Our soul is the "thumbprint" of God. Our soul is what distinguishes us from the animal kingdom. Our soul allows us to long for eternity. It is like a compass needle aching to point and return to its Creator.

During our earthly pilgrimage, the union of mortal body and immortal soul is significant and interactive. The Romans spoke of a sound mind in a sound body. Joy and sorrow, spiritual though they be, affect our body. Illness and trauma and physical health can depress or elate us. We then communicate these mental and sometimes abstract ideas and thoughts from our soul to our body. Our body becomes the medium of transmission of our mind's content. We are now communicating, in union with the recipient.

Communicating the Word

Logos is Greek for "word," and it has a long and distinguished history. It meant the spoken word or a mediator for pagan gods. For us Christians, it soars to eagle heights when John's gospel begins with the statement: "In the beginning was the Word…." The reference is clearly to the Son of God, who, incarnate, became the visible Word uttered by the Father from all eternity.

When we communicate with another we do not think of the process. It is second nature, automatic. The medium can be a gesture, an embrace, a smile, a frown, a spoken word. The route goes from our mind to our body to another's body and ultimately to the mind, heart, and soul of the hearer or reader.

In this chapter, I am attempting to incarnate my thoughts by making them visible through the written word. As you read them, I hope the physical and perceivable signs will be translated into meaning and you will understand what I am saying. We move from my mind to my fingers to your eyes and, hopefully, to your mind and heart. Voila!

Scripture's journey is from God to the inspired writer to the text to our eyes or ears and to the very depths of our souls. We receive a precious gift.

For the purposes of this discussion, "word of God" will refer to the inspired books of the Bible as defined by the Council of Trent (1546). It includes the books of the Old Testament, beginning with the Book of Genesis, to the Book of Revelation in the New Testament. This is not to imply that God cannot continue to reveal to private individuals, but such revelations must be authenticated by the Church.

The *Dogmatic Constitution on Divine Revelation* reminds us that the two streams of divine revelation are Scripture and Tradition with a capital T. "There exists a close connection and communication between sacred tradition and Sacred Scripture. For both of them, flowing from the same divine wellspring, in a certain way merge into a unity and tend toward the same end…Therefore both sacred tradition and Sacred Scripture are to be accepted and venerated with the same sense of loyalty and reverence" (n. 9).

The Word of God as Gift

When you hear the word *gift*, what comes to mind? Sometimes I think of the frustrated and not too joyful crowds at our malls at holiday time. I am desperate to get a gift for Aunt Mathilda. She will be hurt if I don't, yet she is so hard to buy for. She has everything!

But I also think of the many gifts I have received that were chosen thoughtfully and unexpectedly. For me, the most meaningful gifts are those that are unmerited and given out of sheer love with no return expected.

Every gift is a form of communication. It makes a statement of some sort. But every communication is not necessarily a communication of love. "Pass the salt" expresses my need and my hope that somebody will hear me. It does not imply a strong bond between the hearer and me. The so-called corporate gift (send them all the fruit basket) may express gratitude but not necessarily affection.

So why do we dare to call the Word of God "gift"? Certainly Christ's redemptive life, death, and Resurrection are easily seen as salvific gift. Every Christmas present contains that idea whether consciously or unconsciously.

But is every gift from God an *intimate* gift? It is not too difficult to consider revelation as a gift. It is a gift-giving communication that furthers intimacy. God is sharing secrets!

Intimacy and the Word

In our lives we have family, friends, intimates, and acquaintances. We pass strangers on the street. As children of God, all of these people are our brothers and sisters. But we dare not embrace each and every one of them for fear of being misunderstood and carted off to jail. We may be showing a degree of intimacy that the recipient considers unwelcome.

Intimacy is all about the ability to love and be loved. It is about disclosure without fear of rejection. It is also about commitment. It is a two-way street. The lover reveals himself and does so as a proof of that love. The sharing strengthens the bond. "In his goodness and wisdom God chose to reveal himself and to make known to us the hidden purpose of his will…Through this revelation, therefore, the invisible God…out of the abundance of his love speaks to men as friends…and lives among them" (*Dogmatic Constitution on Divine Revelation*, n. 2).

So often we use words without thinking of their deeper meaning. We describe an intimate person in our life as a "soul mate." We prefer their physical presence, but physical distance does not destroy the intimacy. Our spirits remain united. Absence can make the heart grow fonder and increase the joy of physical reunion. Our soul can grow stronger or, alas, weaker.

This Gratuitous Communication

Eucharist is food for our journey, lest, because of malnutrition, we falter and fall. Extraordinary Synod XI called by Pope Benedict XVI in 2005 was on the Eucharist. Three years later, he convened Synod XII. Its topic was the Word of God. Before a synod meets, a document called *Lineamenta* is circulated among the bishops. The document contains topics and questions for discussion. The bishops and theologians then send in their reactions. After the synod, a statement is issued.

In the *Lineamenta* for the synod on the Word of God, we read: "This Synod wishes to set forth, in continuity with the preceding one, the intrinsic connection between the Eucharist and the word of God, since the Church must receive nourishment from the one 'bread of life from the table of both God's word and Christ's body.' This is the Synod's underlying purpose and primary goal, namely, to fully encounter the Word of God in Jesus the Lord, present in the Sacred Scriptures and the Eucharist. St. Jerome observes: 'The Lord's flesh is real food and his blood real drink: this is our true good in this present life: to nourish ourselves with his flesh and to drink his blood in not only the Eucharist but also the reading of Sacred Scripture. In fact, the Word of God, drawn from the knowledge of the Scriptures, is real food and real drink'" (Introduction, n. 4).

Further on we read: "This gratuitous communication, which presupposes a deep communion analogous to human intimacy, is characterized by God himself and his Word, that is the 'Word of God'" (I, n. 6).

At the Table

One of the great gifts that fosters human intimacy is dining together. Having a meal with loved ones can be a sublime experience. Coming from an Italian family, I recall with great joy meals where we didn't want to leave and break the spell. Both the company and the cuisine drew us to remain.

The Old Testament speaks of the joys of the table. Christ taught at table. Heaven is described as a banquet. At Eucharist we have the two tables with awesome gifts: the table of the Word and the table of the Eucharist. Both communicate love and intimacy. But we can also partake one on one with the Scripture just by picking up our Bible. Scripture is a treasure chest of gifts waiting to be opened.

We live in a nation of fast food dining. But the word should not be gulped down. Just as elegant food takes time to prepare, we should take our time to relish it in order to get its full benefit. When this idea is applied to the word of God, we call it *lectio divina*.

> At Eucharist we have the two tables with awesome gifts: the table of the Word and the table of the Eucharist. Both communicate love and intimacy.

In his Angelus address, November 6, 2005, Pope Benedict said, *lectio divina* "consists in poring over a biblical text for some time, reading it and rereading it, as it were, 'ruminating' on it as the Fathers say and squeezing from it, so to speak, all its 'juice' so that it may nourish meditation and contemplation and, like water, succeed in irrigating life itself.'

The Scriptures will never run out of juice. Nor should we ever not be thirsty.

Conclusion

We have briefly considered the Word of God as gift. It is humbling that our Creator should give creatures gifts so sublime, or that he should wish to have an intimate relationship with us. What can we give in return?

In the Third Eucharistic Prayer we ask God that Christ may "make of us an everlasting offering to you." Not really a fair exchange! He gives us everything, we give him ourselves. And we need his help to do so. The Scriptures are a love letter from God. Lovers cherish communications and gifts from the beloved. We cherish this revelation and should be astonished that he wants us to get to know him and his plan for history.

If catechists have fire in their bellies and hearts filled with hunger and love for the Word, then, with God's help, students will catch the spark. As grateful recipients of the gift, they will joyfully share it with others.

Your Thoughts

1 What does the reception of a gift mean in my life? When are gifts most meaningful? Why?

____

____

2 What is my understanding of "soul"? Has it changed over the years? What questions or issues still remain when I talk with others about the spiritual life and the soul?

____

____

Try This

If _lectio divina_ is part of your spiritual journey, share your experience with a neighbor, friend, or student. Explain to that person how _lectio divina_ is an opportunity to experience the Word of God as gift. If you are not familiar with the methodology of _lectio divina,_ search the term on the internet for copious resources.

3

ECUMENICAL, INTERRELIGIOUS, *and* CULTURAL DIALOGUE

SR. ANGELA ANN ZUKOWSKI, MHSH

More often than not, Catholics who grew up pre-Vatican II recall the family Bible as a sacred book containing the names and dates of births, deaths, and sacramental moments in the family. Seldom do they recall that family Bible opened for reading, reflection, and prayer. As a matter of fact, it was perceived that reading the Bible was a Protestant—not Catholic—activity.

In 1943, Pope Pius XII's encyclical *Divino Afflante Spiritu* ("Inspired by the Divine Spirit") paved the way for biblical renewal within the Church. Catholic biblical scholars embraced the new biblical renewal.

Subsequently, the Second Vatican Council created a new threshold for the Scriptures; nevertheless, adult faith formation had not taken hold within our parishes to implement the recommendations found in the *Dogmatic Constitution on Divine Revelation.*

The most significant change emerged in catechetical materials with lesson plans that wove Scripture into elementary and secondary text-books. Each lesson was to reflect a dimension of doctrine, Scripture, liturgy, and witness. Identifying a biblical passage that could connect with the doctrinal theme was the primary focus for incorporating the Scriptures.

The emergence of vacation Bible school programs animated more biblical enthusiasm as creative activities, exercises, and skits breathed life into the biblical stories. While some VBS may have established a more solid biblical curriculum that transcended a superficial collage of biblical understanding and appreciation, the VBS was a fun program to keep children entertained during the summer months.

The Struggle with Biblical Illiteracy

The Catholic marketplace gradually incorporated Scripture study programs with a plethora of self-study materials, popular approaches to the Bible, and the vast assortment of Catholic biblical scholarly publications. We seemed well on our way.

In spite of it all, however, surveys show that Catholics still struggled with biblical illiteracy—and this reality did not go unnoticed by Pope Benedict XVI. He called for the 2008 Synod of Bishops General Assembly to animate Catholic biblical consciousness, study, and integration into the life of the Church.

The synod bishops focused their attention on a prepared working document called an *Instrumentum Laboris* entitled "The Word of God in the Life and Mission of the Church." This document outlines the expectations and desired outcomes of the synod. Four of the eleven expectations connect with this book, and the last point particularly has influenced this chapter:

- The word of God needs to be given greater priority in the life and mission of the Church.

- The Bible needs to be seen as the Word of God who continues to reveal.

- The laity urgently need to be aware that they are not passive objects in relation to the Word of God.

- The Word seeks a dialogue within the Church, with Christian communities, with other religions, and even with culture—always mindful of the many seeds of truth that God's providence has placed in them.

The Importance of Dialogue

Dialogue is a way of encountering and understanding oneself and the world at the deepest level, opening up possibilities of grasping the fundamental meaning of life (individually and collectively) and its various dimensions.

This in turn transforms the way we deal with ourselves, others, and the world. Indeed, the word *dialogue*, in theory, most appropriately describes the nature of a meeting of minds. Dialogue is not the only way that individuals or groups interact—but dialogue is indispensable for inner peace and peace in the world.

Over the years the Church has produced copious documents that call for authentic interreligious dialogue. Pope Paul VI's 1964 encyclical, *Ecclesiam suam* ("Paths of the Church"), articulated the characteristics of dialogue: (1) clarity: what is explained must be intelligible; (2) we must lead dialogue in the spirit of Christ, which is meekness; (3) trust is necessary in both partners of dialogue; (4) prudence takes into account the moral and psychological circumstances of the conversation partner.

The Nature of Dialogue

Dialogue draws life from friendly relations and service. Genuine dialogue aims at listening and learning from each of the conversation partners. Obviously, we need not adopt an uncritical attitude in relation to other religions. But we can open ourselves to their spiritual and moral values and join them in defending religious liberty, social welfare, and peace.

Therefore, when the synod bishops call us to cultivate the principles of dialogue, they believe that a thorough, well-grounded, and lifelong program of biblical studies can enable us to enter into genuine dialogue with women and men of other traditions.

Indeed, this is no small task. It is far too simple for Catholics to fall into the trap of biblical fundamentalism. The bishops encourage us to become more mature in authentic biblical comprehension, grounding ourselves in the breadth and depth of biblical studies. Only then are we prepared for serious conversations that set the stage for quality interreligious and ecumenical dialogue.

The Religious Contexts for Dialogue

Interfaith dialogue is most challenging because the differences between religious traditions are so basic, influencing personal and social identity and behavior in untold ways. It is most important because interreligious relationships have frequently been marked by hostility.

The opportunity to cultivate interreligious dialogue rooted in the Scriptures is not only for ideological and biblical comparison but it also enables a true encounter between those spiritual insights and experiences that are found only at the deepest levels of human life. Of all the documents from the Second Vatican Council, *Nostra Aetate* ("Declaration on the Relation of the Church to Non-Christian Religions") is held as the keystone for confirming movement toward meaningful dialogue.

The synod bishops affirmed that the faith that unites us is an invitation to discuss together the differences in interpreting the living word of God that we share, while reflecting on the reasons responsible for the divisions that divide us.

At the same time, progress made in ecumenical dialogue with the

> The dialogue between Christians and people of other living faiths is, in certain respects, the most challenging and most important frontier in the Church's dialogue.

word of God can undoubtedly lead to other benefits. According to the Second Vatican Council, "this change of heart and holiness of life, along with public and private prayer for the unity of Christians, should be regarded as the soul of the whole ecumenical movement" (*Decree on Ecumenism,* n. 8).

According to Pope Benedict XVI: "Listening to the Word of God is a priority for our ecumenical commitment. Indeed, it is not we who act or who organize the unity of the Church. The Church does not make herself or live of herself, but from the creative Word that comes from the mouth of God" ("The Word of God in the Life and Mission of the Church," n. 27).

The Impact for Catechesis

Every media outlet carries religious stories that have an impact on our awareness of the shrinking global village. We are coming face to face with Jewish, Muslim, Buddhist, Hindu, and other forms of religious expression woven into our political, social, and economic realities. Whether we are conscious of them or not, they have an impact on our religious perspective with regard to how we define the religious tradition in question *and* our interpretation and response to them.

All too often our ignorance can substitute "caricatures and stereotypes for inaccurate information" (*National Directory for Catechesis,* n. 51D). We cannot escape the encounter, the challenges, and the opportunities these events open to us. Nevertheless, we need to be well prepared to engage in the dialogue without falling prey to syncretism, superficial approaches, or distortion of the truth.

> We need to be well prepared to engage in the dialogue without falling prey to syncretism, superficial approaches, or distortion of the truth.

The *National Directory for Catechesis* (NDC) states that catechesis "should aim to form a genuine ecumenical attitude in those being catechized, to foster ecumenism" (51B). The NDC refers to the *Directory for the Application of Principles and Norms of Ecumenism*, identifying some key elements in ecumenical formation of catechists: 1) careful study of sacred Scripture and the Church's living Tradition; 2) familiarity with the biblical foundations of ecumenism; 3) familiarity with Catholic principles of ecumenism; 4) knowledge of the history of ecumenism; 5) training in ecumenical collaboration and dialogue; 6) participation in visits to other churches, informal exchanges, joint study days, and common prayer; 7) experience in ecumenical collaboration and dialogue; and 8) familiarity with fundamental ecumenical issues (NDC, n. 51C).

" [M]any Christians do not have a fundamental understanding of the history and traditions of Judaism" (NDC, n. 51D). Therefore our catechesis must prepare our students for objectivity as well as understanding and dialogue. In referencing *God's Mercy Endures Forever: Guidelines on the Presentation of Jews and Judaism in Catholic Preaching*, the NDC encourages catechists to: 1) affirm the value of the whole Bible, both Old and New Testaments, and recognize the special meaning of the Old Testament for the Jewish people, its original audience; 2) show both the independence and the interconnectedness of the Old and the New Testament; 3) emphasize the Jewishness of Jesus and his teachings; and 4) respect the continuing existence of God's covenant with the Jewish people and their faithful response, despite centuries of suffering, to God's call (n. 51D).

Preparing for the Encounter

The objective of this chapter is simply to set the stage for awakening catechists to the importance of a solid biblical foundation for effectively entering into a meaningful interreligious or ecumenical dialogue, or for designing catechetical experiences to prepare their students for the encounter. Just as Jesus Christ touches the human heart through dialogue, so too, Christian disciples, empowered by the Spirit of Christ, should pursue sincere and patient dialogue with people of differing religious beliefs or traditions.

By establishing a solid biblical foundation within in the lives of students, catechists set the stage for empowering them to love the Scriptures and discover within them the seeds for worthwhile ecumenical and interreligious dialogue. Catechists are called to cultivate their catechetical commitment and the whole of their lives rooted in the Scriptures; thus, they are prepared to dialogue, effectively and compassionately, with other religious traditions in the search for nurturing a culture of peace, justice, and love.

Conclusion

German Cardinal Walter Kasper is one of the most significant ecumenical leaders in the Catholic Church. His writings have been the benchmark for those seriously interested in advancing dialogue with diverse religious traditions and cultures. We close with his prophetic insight written in February, 2003:

"If you had asked passers-by in West Berlin on the morning of 9 November 1989, 'How much longer do you think the wall will remain standing?', the majority would surely have replied, 'We would be happy if our grandchildren pass through the Brandenburg Gate one day.' On the evening of that memorable day the world witnessed something totally unexpected in Berlin. It is my firm conviction that one day too we will rub our eyes in amazement that God's Spirit has broken through the seemingly insurmountable walls that divide us and given us new ways through to each other and to a new full communion" ("Reflections by Card. Walter Kasper: Nature and Purpose of Ecumenical Dialogue").

Your Thoughts

1 Is there a difference between dialogue, discussion, and debate? What has been my experience of all three?

____

____

2 What impact do contemporary media have on my understanding or appreciation of other religious traditions?

____

____

Try This

- Explore the internet to identify Catholic biblical study programs. What appear to be their strengths and weaknesses?

- Read one of the Church documents referenced in this article. What new insights can have an impact on your catechetical lesson planning?

4

The WORD *of* GOD *and the* EUCHARIST

WILLIAM P. ROBERTS

But it was only in the breaking of the bread that their eyes were opened and they recognized him. Then they commented to each other, "Were not our hearts burning [within us] while he spoke to us on the way, and opened the Scriptures to us?" (LUKE 24: 32)

Christria Present Today

The familiar post-Resurrection narrative of the disciples on the road to Emmaus tells us that Christ relates to the disciples through Scripture and the breaking of the bread. This, then, serves as an appropriate background for reflecting on how Christ continues to communicate himself to us in Word and in Eucharist. In this chapter, we will reflect on his unique presence in the Liturgy of the Word and in the Eucharist, the relationship of both of these presences to each other, and some of the applications that flow from this.

Christ's Presence in the Liturgy of the Word

The first belief we bring to the Eucharist is that Christ is the Word of God. The prologue in John's gospel gives clear testimony to this article of faith: "In the beginning was the Word, and the Word was with God, and the Word was God....And the Word became flesh and made his dwelling among us, and we saw his glory, the glory as of the Father's only Son, full of grace and truth" (John 1:1, 14).

The Letter to the Hebrews sees Christ as the fulfillment of God's self-communication to humans: "In times past, God spoke in partial and various ways to our ancestors through the prophets; in these last days he spoke to us through a son, whom he made heir of all things and through whom he created the universe, who is the refulgence of his glory, the very imprint of his being, and who sustains all things by his mighty word" (1:1–3).

We come to the Liturgy of the Word not just to hear words about Christ but to open ourselves to the Real Presence of Christ who speaks to us now through the reading of the Scriptures. We allow Christ, the Word of God, to encounter us and to transform us.

The connection between receiving the Word of God and eating is also brought out elsewhere in the Scriptures. When God sent the prophet Ezekiel to speak to the people, a written scroll "covered with writing front and back" is unrolled before him (Ezekiel 2:10). God then said to Ezekiel, "Son of man, eat what you find here: eat this scroll, then go, speak to the house of Israel. So I opened my mouth and he gave me the scroll to eat" (3:1–2).

> Like Ezekiel, we must absorb the Word of God into our being in order to be enlightened and empowered to communicate this Word effectively to others.

At the Liturgy of the Word we are called not just to hear God's Word but to eat it, drink it in, let it enter into our minds, our hearts, our souls; to integrate it into the depths of our being so that it transforms us and becomes the inspiration for the way we live and relate to God and to others. This is of vital necessity for all of us Christians, but especially teachers, preachers, catechists, and parents. Like Ezekiel, we must absorb the Word of God into our being in order to be enlightened and empowered to communicate this Word effectively to others.

The inner connection between the Word and the Eucharist is also brought out in John's gospel. It is in the context of the multiplication of the loaves that John situates Jesus' Bread of Life discourse. For John, Jesus is the Bread of Life in a double sense. "I am the bread of life; whoever comes to me will never hunger, and whoever *believes* in me will never thirst....For this is the will of my Father, that everyone who sees the Son and *believes* in him may have eternal life, and I shall raise him [on] the last day" (John 6:35, 40, emphases mine).

Then later Jesus proclaims: "I am the bread of life. Your ancestors ate the manna in the desert, but they died; this is the bread that comes down from heaven so that one may eat it and not die. I am the living bread that came down from heaven; whoever eats this bread will live forever; and the bread that I will give is my flesh for the life of the world....Whoever eats my flesh and drinks my blood has eternal life, and I will raise him on the last day. For my flesh is true food, and my blood is true drink. Whoever eats my flesh and drinks my blood remains in me and I in him" (6:48–51, 54–56).

Having reflected on Jesus as the Bread of Life in the Liturgy of the Word, we now turn to considering Jesus, the Bread of Life in the Eucharist.

Christ's Presence in the Liturgy of the Eucharist

Our ultimate liturgical response to the Liturgy of the Word is the Liturgy of the Eucharist. This includes the Presentation of the Gifts, the Eucharistic Prayer, and Communion.

The Presentation of the Gifts: At the Presentation of the Gifts we bring forth our gifts of bread and wine as a symbol of the other offerings we contribute for the well-being and mission of our parish community. More deeply, we bring these gifts as a sacramental sign of the offering of our lives and the way we strive to live in the Spirit of Christ. With the celebrant, we raise these gifts toward God, praising the God of all creation through whose goodness we have this bread and wine to offer. We pray that they may become our bread of life and spiritual drink. We then affirm this offering with the response, "Blessed be God for ever."

The Eucharistic Prayer: In the Eucharistic Prayer, at the words of consecration, Christ, through the priest, proclaims the gift of himself to us as he did at the Last Supper and enacted on the cross: "Take this, all of you, and eat of it, for this is my body, which will be given up for you…Take this, all of you, and drink from it, for this is the chalice of my blood, the blood of the new and eternal covenant, which will be poured out for you and for many for the forgiveness of sins."

As these words are proclaimed, we acknowledge in mind and heart Christ's unique presence and self-offering. "Save us, Savior of the world, for by your Cross and Resurrection, you have set us free." We are also reminded that this is the model for Christian living: to share our bread and wine with others; to give of our bodies, our blood, our talents, our personal gifts to nurture and enhance the lives of others; and to make the world a better place for all.

Communion: At Communion, in the most visible (sacramental) way possible, we express our desire and our openness to Christ, the Incarnate Word, the crucified and risen One, to enter ever further into the depths of our being to transform our minds, our hearts, and our souls into his image. We eat this Eucharistic bread and drink this Eucharistic wine as the most explicit way we have of symbolizing our need and our yearning for Christ to be in us and with us.

We say "Amen" to Christ's gift of his risen Body, his Blood (his life), so that we might deepen our baptismal participation in the death and resurrection of Jesus (see Romans 6:3–11). In receiving this bread and wine as a sacrament of the unique presence of Christ, we proclaim in the most liturgical way we can, "Come, Lord Jesus" (see Revelation 22:20).

In Memory of Me

At the conclusion of Jesus' Eucharistic proclamation, he exhorts us, "Do this in memory of me." The first obvious way we fulfill this command is by liturgically celebrating the Eucharist. Nevertheless, there is a deeper meaning of doing Eucharist in memory of Christ.

We are challenged to go forth from the liturgy and make Christ present in our lives. We do this by the way we regard and treat other people. We are called to become the body of Christ for others. We become his hands by giving bread to the hungry, drink to the thirsty, and clothes to the naked.

We bring his hope and new life to the underprivileged by visiting the sick and the imprisoned, by sheltering the homeless, and by providing refuge for the immigrant, the oppressed, and the enslaved.

We make his presence felt in the lives of our family and all those whom we contact by allowing his kingdom of truth, life, love, justice, and peacemaking to reign in all of our relationships.

Conclusion

Christ came as the Word of God incarnate. He continues to proclaim his Word to us especially in the Liturgy of the Word. He is present to us most sacramentally in the giving of himself in Eucharist. We who listen to his Word and receive him in Eucharist are sent forth to be for others the Body of Christ, the One who comes to serve, not to be served.

Your Thoughts

1 Has the story of the Emmaus experience connected with me? How? Why?

____

____

2 What are some of the practical ways in which I can live Eucharist more fully in my family, among my friendships, and in my service to others?

____

____

Try This

Read Matthew 25:31–46. Here Matthew unfolds what the Church calls the Spiritual and Corporal Works of Mercy. How are these exercised in your life? Reflect on how you can animate your students to practice and become witnesses to these works of mercy in concrete ways every day of their lives.

STUDYING *and* INTERPRETING SCRIPTURE

SUE GRENOUGH

"Their [catechists] proclamation of the Gospel, their personal testimony, and their living witness to the transcendent values of the Christian life can be particularly effective because they know the ordinary experiences of everyday life so well and are able to incarnate the Gospel in those ordinary circumstances." **NATIONAL DIRECTORY FOR CATECHESIS, N. 54B, 8**

Living and Sharing the Word

It is an awesome and significant responsibility of those who serve as ministers to God's people to be effective and faithful to living and sharing the word of God. We must carefully read, study, pray, and be versed in interpreting the sacred texts. The ministers of God's people must steep themselves in the word of God.

What does this call for? The word *steep* brings to mind the image of making a good cup of tea and the experience of drinking it. The process cannot be rushed. Making tea takes time, patience, and planning. There is the choice of which flavor to prepare. The water must be boiled, and the tea must be steeped in the water. And then, when ready, the tea is enjoyed by sipping slowly.

The approach to Scripture is very much like making tea. We have to set aside time for the study and reading of the sacred text. We have to plan which book or selection of the Bible to study. And a good reflective environment will help us become steeped (immersed) in God's sacred word.

Why Study the Word?

Because we are encouraged to read the sacred word of God, some wonder why there is a need to study and interpret it. Doesn't the word speak for itself? Doesn't the need to study make it less available to the faithful?

First, there is no doubt that the reading of Scripture is grace-filled, as the word of God reveals God and is the presence of God. Second, as we desire to probe and understand further the meaning of the word, study is as necessary in the approach to Scripture as it is for any other type of literature we read. The purpose for which it was written and the context and culture of the times are information that will enlighten us to a greater depth of understanding.

Any time we read a work of literature, it is important to know whether it is fiction, nonfiction, history, science, poetry, etc., because the form of the written word helps determine meaning. The customs, concerns, and way of life of the people of a certain time and location will influence the images and language used.

From this information, Scripture scholars discern the truth "God wanted to communicate to us" (DV, n. 12). Then the interpretation of Scripture is subject to "the judgment of the Church, which carries out the divine commission and ministry of guarding and interpreting the word of God" (DV, n.12). It is important to remember that the interpretation must always reflect the content and unity of the whole of Scripture. There is an integrity and harmony in the truths of Scripture, which is what the exegetes of Scripture work to maintain (see DV, n.12).

Also, we need to study Scripture because we can easily rely on our perceptions and let our familiarity with many of the stories of Scripture lull us into thinking that we know the meanings of the language, culture, and context. Some of these perceptions can even exist as accepted myths.

For example, respond to the following five statements as true or false:

1. The books of the Bible were written in the order in which they appear, i.e., Genesis, Exodus, Leviticus, etc.

2. The stories of Scripture, for the most part, were written when they occurred.

3. The Church possesses the original texts of the Bible.

4. There are no contradictions in Scripture.

5. One author wrote an entire book.

Correct responses:
1. False: The books of the Bible are not arranged in chronological order. The dating is more complicated than that, and the dates for many books are given as possible ranges of years rather than specific dates.

2. False: The events that are recorded in the Bible were communicated orally for years before the final writing, editing, and acceptance into the canon of the Bible. Most people at the time of the events could not read or write.

3. False: We do not have any original texts of the Bible. We have early fragments and we are always working with translations of translations, which can be difficult, as words often do not translate easily into other languages.

4. False: There are many contradictions in Scripture—that is, similar accounts that do not match exactly. The order of creation in Genesis chapter 1 and chapter 2 is an example. Another example concerns the details of the conversion of Paul in the Acts of the Apostles.

5. False: The first step in the composition of any of the sacred texts was the oral telling of the story/event. Writing came later. Usually there were many authors and editors until the final editor put the various stories and traditions together into a final book for acceptance into the canon, the officially accepted books considered inspired and normative.

These five often-accepted myths serve as some of the reasons why reliance on Scripture scholars for the study and interpretation of Scripture is needed for authentic reading. Those experienced in the study of the cultures, times, and languages in which the various books of the Bible were written offer us the background we need to read Scripture with insight and understanding.

We need not be deterred from approaching Scripture; nor should we be simplistic in our approach to Scripture. Instead, this information can and should prompt us to rely on the guidance of the Church when approaching Scripture.

The Teaching Office of the Church

"The task of authentically interpreting the word of God, whether written or handed on, has been entrusted exclusively to the living teaching office of the Church, whose authority is exercised in the name of Jesus Christ" (DV, n. 10). This can give us confidence and assurance. Humility and a mind and heart open to the guidance of the Holy Spirit are required for the study of Scripture. If few are able to study Shakespeare without assistance, one should not be surprised that Scripture, which is literature even more ancient, would also need commentaries, dictionaries, and summaries.

In the ministry of the word, various Church documents call for formation in Scripture for Church ministers. The *General Directory for Catechesis* says, "Sacred Scripture should be the very soul" of the formation of catechists (n. 240). The *National Directory for Catechesis* states that catechists must be firmly rooted in sacred Scripture (n. 55E). How does a catechist proceed in this study? Some background information can be helpful.

First, if we have an acquaintance with types of literature, we can more easily appreciate the significance of this in the various books of the Bible. Knowing what form of literature is used and why it was used will give some insight into the message of the written work. Then theological errors can more easily be avoided. For instance, one won't be tempted to read Genesis as scientific evidence regarding the beginning of the world when we know that the book was written as poetry expressing the religious origins of creation and the goodness of the Creator revealed in all of it.

> Knowing what form of literature is used and why it was used will give some insight into the message of the written work.

Second, understanding similarities and differences in the cultures of the Middle East can prepare us for meeting a different culture and time in the stories of our spiritual ancestors. The appreciation of the similar essential questions about the mysteries of life and death that are part of the faith journey will be found in the people of ancient times as well as in people today.

Skills for Scripture Study

For our personal faith, study of the Scriptures can occur through individual study, in a group, or in a more formal class setting. The goal of steeping ourselves in God's word is to nourish our faith so that our words and life make God visible in everyday life. There are some skills we can develop to make this a reality.

First: Make the reading of Scripture a frequent if not daily habit.

Second: It is very important to read the introduction to each book of the

Bible as well as the footnotes. These sources of information are valuable for the context of the reading.

Third: Make use of the wisdom of Catholic Scripture scholars by referencing a commentary and/or a dictionary.

Fourth: Read more than the lectionary selections. Read an entire chapter or, better, an entire book. Then the hearing of the lectionary selections during Mass will have the added significance of the context in which they occur.

As we steep ourselves in the Scriptures in these ways, these practices will filter down to those to whom we minister. If we exhibit ease with approaching the sacred texts for nourishment and guidance, the faithful entrusted to our care will be encouraged to use the Scriptures for their own benefit as well.

Guiding the faithful to read the information about the books in the Bible through the introductions and footnotes will help develop the appropriate reading habits for Scripture. Investigate together the customs and concerns of the people of another time and place, and discover together God's care and mercy for humankind. What we practice regarding Scripture for ourselves will be the same traits we encourage and pass on to the faithful.

Conclusion

Developing skills for reading Scripture and habits of studying Scripture fulfills the role that is shared by the community entrusted with the word of God. The community is to pray, study, celebrate, and pass on God's word so that it may come to know God more authentically through God's own revelation—and know hope. The Word of God is the very presence of God. "For whatever was written previously was written for our instruction, that by endurance and by the encouragement of the scriptures we might have hope" (Romans 15:4).

Your Thoughts

1 How does the metaphor of steeping tea relate to my approach to the study of Scripture?

____

____

____

2 How do I prioritize and set the stage for my study of Scripture? Or what adaptations can I make to begin the journey?

____

____

____

Try This

Search the internet for "Catholic biblical studies" to discover a wealth of catechetical materials for your ongoing biblical studies. Prepare a file of these resources for future reference.

SCRIPTURE *and* MARY *of* NAZARETH

FR. BERTRAND BUBY, SM

*The **Dogmatic Constitution on Divine Revelation** serves as the
background for praying, studying, researching, teaching, and writing about
Scripture as the word of God. **The Dogmatic Constitution on the Church**,
chapter eight, is the Vatican II document on Mary. These two documents
enable us to reflect on New Testament texts that refer to Mary.*

The Mother of Jesus

The gospels of John and Luke, plus Luke's Acts of the Apostles, are the
primary biblical sources for the relationship of God's revelatory word and
Mary. Both inspired writers were aware of the warm relationship their
communities had with the mother of Jesus. Both are theologians and
evangelists of incarnational theology. This is evident in the Prologue of
John (John 1:1–18) and in the Annunciation account of Luke (1:26–38).

Mary, more than any other woman in the New Testament, is mentioned in all four gospels and in the Acts of the Apostles. There may be other indirect or symbolic recollections of her in Paul and in the Apocalypse or Book of Revelation.

John's Gospel: A Gospel of Revelation

The Prologue of John's gospel is the most sublime introduction and overture that we have of the relationship of the word of God to all believers, and especially through the living example of the "mother of Jesus"—John's favorite title for Mary. As we read and ponder over verse 14 of the Prologue, we enter into incarnational theology and spirituality, and we experience "the Word became flesh and made his dwelling among us, and we saw his glory, the glory as of the Father's only Son, full of grace and truth" (1:14). With that scriptural and incarnational verse, we are assured that there is a special role for Mary in salvation history.

The mother of Jesus was there and Jesus was also invited. John 2:1–12 tells us that Mary is present at the beginning of Jesus' active ministry at the wedding feast at Cana. She also will be with Jesus in his last hour as he dies upon the cross. Thus, John frames the life of Jesus with a scene at the beginning, in which Mary is central, and at the end of Jesus' life, as he breathes forth his Spirit upon his mother and on the beloved disciple (see John 19:25–27).

At Cana, Mary initiates the "hour" of Jesus by acting as a catalyst who makes him aware of the needs of the couple and their family members once the wine has run short. Her words are brief but effective and symbolic: "They have no wine." Then she speaks directly to the servants: "Do whatever he tells you."

> Making known the needs of those responsible for the feast shows Mary's trust in her son and her belief in his very person as someone who can do what God would do.

Once this is done, Jesus changes the water in the six huge jars into precious wine, thereby showing the power of his words and his ability to listen to the needs of others expressed by his mother. The symbols of the water and wine remind us of our own faith pondering the sacrament of baptism and the sacrament of the Eucharist.

Making known the needs of those responsible for the feast shows Mary's trust in her son and her belief in his very person as someone who can do what God would do. Her words are meant for us; we are to do whatever Jesus tells us. Jesus anticipates his "hour," which we will come to realize means his suffering, death, and resurrection in this gospel of revelation.

Mary thus is the initiator of the first sign of seven in this gospel. Her profound faith in Jesus results in an act of hospitality and kindness on a joyous occasion. Now Jesus' active ministry is set in motion to accomplish God's plan of salvation for humanity, then and in succeeding ages. Not only has the mother of Jesus demonstrated her belief in the power of Jesus' word, but she also leads his disciples to believe in him and his word: "and his disciples began to believe in him. After this, he and his mother, [his] brothers, and his disciples went down to Capernaum…" (John 2:11–12).

Mary and the beloved disciple at the foot of the cross The symbolism and the themes present in the Cana account are now fully realized in the revelatory text of John 19:25–28: "Standing by the cross of Jesus were his mother and his mother's sister, Mary the wife of Clopas, and Mary of Magdala. When Jesus saw his mother and the disciple there whom he loved, he said to his mother, 'Woman, behold, your son.' Then he said to the disciple, 'Behold, your mother.' And from that hour the disciple took her into his home. After this, aware that everything was now finished, in order that the scripture might be fulfilled, Jesus said, 'I thirst.'"

Here, the most solemn meaning of the "hour" of Jesus takes place with the three women at the foot of the cross and the beloved disciple standing next to Mary, one of the three women who is singled out for a special mission as the mother of Jesus. She is a courageous woman who has remained faithful to the person of her son. She is witness to his surrendering of his body to God. More than the others, Mary hands over the flesh that she had engendered for God as Jesus returns to the Father.

This is John's Pentecostal scene, wherein the Church has its origins—

at the foot of the Cross. It is born of the water (baptism) and the blood (Eucharist) that flow from the side of Jesus. These two precious elements had been foreshadowed at Cana through the water being changed into wine, the blood of the grape and symbol for the Eucharist.

Indeed, the Fourth Gospel is the revelatory word, Jesus, saying these last words of love to his mother and to the beloved disciple whom our tradition tells us is John. The scene is both theological and intimately human. It is one of tenderness and filial love. It is above all a fulfillment of the loving covenant God gave us through the Son; it is the mission of Jesus completed in a revelation of humankind's salvation.

Luke and the Virgin Mary and the Word of God

Luke the Evangelist is multitalented as a theologian, a historian, and a literary artist who paints the portrait of Mary so well that she speaks from the framework of his gospel.

We have a wealth of revelatory words of God in the first two chapters of Luke, which we name an "Infancy Gospel" or "Infancy Narrative." As Catholics, especially those devoted to the Rosary, we can easily follow the story of Mary by recalling the Joyful Mysteries of the Rosary, which are taken from the sequence of events about Mary in Luke's introductory chapters. Luke presents Mary as a woman of prayer.

First, she is shown as a person who articulates the promises of God made to his people. Her canticle, the *Magnificat* (see Luke 1:46–55), flows from the inspired words of the Hebrew Scriptures. Her spirit "rejoices in God my Savior" (Habakkuk 3:18). The Lord "has looked upon his handmaid's lowliness" (1 Samuel 1:11). God's name is holy and "his mercy is from age to age to those who fear him" (Psalms 111:9; 103:17). "He has thrown down the rulers from

> We have a wealth of revelatory words of God in the first two chapters of Luke, which we name "Infancy Gospels" or "Infancy Narratives."

their thrones but lifted up the lowly" (Job 5:11; 12:19). She continues to pray, "The hungry he has filled with good things" (Psalm 107:9) and "He has helped Israel his servant, remembering his mercy" (Psalm 98:3; Isaiah 41:8–9).

Second, Mary prays through the profound reflection she gives to the events in which she is involved through salvation history (the Annunciation, the Birth of Jesus, his presentation in the Temple, and when she and Joseph find the young Jesus in the Temple). It is at these moments where Luke uses his phrase about her prayerful heart: "And Mary kept all these things, reflecting on them in her heart" (Luke 2:19). And some dozen years later, at the end of the scene in which Jesus is found in the Temple, she prays again in this reflective mode: "His mother kept all these things in her heart" (Luke 2:51).

Finally, a third form of prayer is described by Luke as the community of the disciples is in the upper room in Jerusalem: "All these devoted themselves with one accord to prayer, together with some women, and Mary the mother of Jesus, and his brothers" (Acts 1:14).

From the moment Mary is introduced in Luke, she is a person who attempts to fathom the mysteries of God within her and those who surround her. She is a reflective person; her prayer is one of biblical reflection.

In the first instance at the Annunciation, she reflects on the meaning of how her son is to be Savior and Messiah-Lord. She does not solve the mystery; she ponders it, attempts to understand it, and "re-members" the events.

Luke has set aside his second reference to Mary's pondering at the end of his considerations of the child's growth into manhood. The verse acts as a conclusion followed by a short transition to what will ensue in the future. Just as Mary is the bridge to the rest of the Gospel, her prayer stance of "pondering with concern" is one that we, as believers and disciples of Jesus, should take to understand the revelation of the beginnings of salvation and the workings of salvation in the person of Jesus the Lord.

Conclusion

Besides our ordinary forms of prayer, we would do well to imitate Mary's pondering in her heart the mysteries of God that are in us and surround us. The sacred Scriptures can be the perfect source for such reflective prayer. To do this, we read the Scriptures carefully, while seeing them within a context. It is only when events and words are grasped in relationship to other events and words that this pondering becomes fruitful.

We need a quiet time and place for the joy and peace of the Spirit to permeate our busy, action-oriented lives. Reflection is the sign of a mature prayer life. Mary is a great biblical model of faith inspiring us to such prayer followed by apostolic action.

Your Thoughts

1 How would I describe my Marian spirituality? What questions or concerns do I hold about the role of Mary in my spiritual life?

____

____

2 What Scripture passages speak to me most profoundly about Mary? Why?

____

____

Try This

Slowly read aloud the *Magnificat*, which is found in Luke 1:46–55. Ponder the phrases and allow your spiritual imagination to capture the breadth and depth of this beautiful prayer. Write a personal reflection on your understanding of the *Magnificat*. Share your reflection with a colleague or friend.

PASTORAL APPLICATIONS

JOYCE M. KELLEHER

This book has been a journey of accessing, experiencing, understanding, celebrating, studying, and listening to the Word of God. This final chapter will focus on applying the word of God to our lives.

Does anyone else know this?

How can we help our students and ourselves become more aware of how the living force of God's word is active in our lives? Let's begin with this true story:

It was the First Sunday of Advent. The children were gathered for their celebration of Liturgy of the Word. The gospel that Sunday told the story of the master who left his servants in charge of the household while he went on a journey (Mark 13:33–37). In this gospel Jesus tells his disciples, "Watch, therefore; you do not know when the lord of the house is coming" (Mark 13:35).

After proclamation of the gospel, the children's lector asked, "What did we hear? What do you think this story can mean?" After some discussion, one child remarked, "I think we are like the servants and Jesus is like the master. We are supposed to take care of things until Jesus comes back."

Upon hearing that, one little boy, about nine years old, jumped up in great excitement and exclaimed, "Is he coming back? Is Jesus coming back?" The children assured him that, indeed, Jesus was coming back as he promised. The boy responded, "Does anyone else know this? Does my mom know this? I can't wait to tell her!"

Does anyone else know this? This was not the child's first exposure to Scripture nor was he new to religious education. By fourth grade, he and his class would have learned about the Second Coming of Jesus. What was it that brought about this discovery and new meaning?

Personally Encountering the Word

Our religion textbooks usually use Scripture to fit the topic of a lesson to be learned. There usually are exercises, questions, and an activity to reinforce the points of the lesson. This approach can be used effectively to teach doctrine, but it has significant limitations if our goal is to help those entrusted to us to apply the word of God to life.

If the textbook method is the only one we use, we risk restricting the meaning of the Scripture passage to just the few points being taught, rather than leaving the dynamic word of God open to speak to us over a lifetime in many different situations. We risk just teaching *about* God instead of creating opportunities to *experience* God. For children especially, this can lead to equating Scripture with their religion textbook that all too often is treated as just another school subject.

Our nine-year-old in this story came to his exciting realization even though he had certainly heard the Scripture before. The difference was the open-ended forum of Liturgy of the Word with Children. For this child, there was the opportunity for conversation, listening to others, mulling over ideas, and then so joyfully coming to his own understanding that he couldn't wait to share it!

This was not a lesson with points to be learned. The children's lector did not try to "teach" the Word or emphasize elements of doctrine. Rather, the lector trusted the power of the word to speak to the children's hearts according to their own needs and on their own timetable.

The work of connecting Scripture to life must be done by those who are living their lives—no one can do it for us. We are the only ones who can bring perceptions of our individual experiences to the word. We cannot do this for others because we do not know what their varied experiences might be.

Only by doing this work ourselves will we learn to make faith-based decisions. Only in this way will we feel and live in God's love, acceptance, and forgiveness as intended for our lives.

Individual Reflection

Catechesis presumes conversion, and conversion presumes that one has heard God's word and responded to it. Therefore, a key element of catechesis for any age is the opportunity for reflection on the word of God, particularly the Sunday gospels.

Whenever possible, individual reflection should be shared with others. When we draw from participants what they hear God saying to them, our method is consistent with the basic Christian belief that each person is a temple of the Holy Spirit, a living source of God's self-revelation (see 1 Corinthians 6:19). This is how we begin to see that God is directly involved in our lives and intimately connected to our everyday experiences.

Lectio Divina

Lectio divina, or "holy reading," is a slow, prayerful way of meditating on Scripture and applying its insights to one's life. It is a treasure of our heritage in which we come to see our personal experiences in light of God's word and apply the word to our lives.

How can we use this method for ourselves and our students? We can simplify the method of *lectio divina* into three steps and models anyone can follow. Ideally, as catechists, we will reflect on the Sunday gospels according to one of these models each week as we prepare for our catechetical sessions. Ideally, as well, we will carve out time at least once each month for our students to reflect with one another during class.

When we use one of these models in a group, it is important to remember to let those entrusted to us arrive at their own insights as to how God is at work in their lives. We can do this by asking open-ended questions rather than by giving answers or telling the participants what they are supposed to get out of the scriptural passage.

It is a moment for us, as catechists, to put aside our teaching role and to become co-listeners. It is an exercise in humility, reminding us that there is only one teacher, the Lord Jesus himself. We must practice getting out of the way so that the word of God can speak.

Model One is best suited for older children and adults who have 30 minutes or more time for reflection.

STEP ONE: GOD'S WORD

1. Read or listen to the Scripture.

2. Reflect on words, phrases, or messages that capture your attention.

3. Imagine yourself in the scene and feel what it is like to be present.

4. *Example:* Read Matthew 8:23–27, which is the story of Jesus and his disciples caught in a storm at sea while Jesus is asleep. What is it like as I imagine myself in the boat? What do I say to Jesus when he asks why I am afraid?

1. Choose several verbs from the passage that captured your attention. Insert them into these questions: (a) When did I/have I ___? What was it like? (b) To whom or with whom did I ___ and how did it feel? (c) Who ___ to me? How did it feel?

2. What insights have I gained from this reflection?

3. *Example:* What is it like for me to be afraid? What are some storms I have faced in life? Who has helped me calm those storms? How has my faith helped me?

STEP THREE: MY RESPONSE

1. What will I do in response to my reflections?

2. What needs to change in my life?

3. What needs to be added to my life?

4. How am I called to be a better disciple in light of the Scripture story and my reflections?

5. *Example:* How can I bring the calming peace of Jesus to those who are afraid? How can I learn to trust more in Jesus' loving care?

Model Two can be used even if older children and adults have just 15 minutes. It is also effective within Liturgy of the Word with Children.

STEP ONE: WHAT DID I HEAR?

Example: In the story of the Last Supper, I imagine myself at the table.

What thoughts, ideas, and feelings do I have as I see Jesus breaking the bread and serving it to me? What do I say to him?

STEP TWO: WHAT DOES THE STORY MEAN TO ME TODAY?
Example: When have I felt as bread broken in my life? When have others broken themselves as bread for me?

STEP THREE: WHAT IS THE STORY ASKING OF ME?
Example: What is Jesus asking of me today? How can I be bread for those who hunger for friendship, food, shelter, forgiveness, and the like?

Model Three is suitable for very young children but can be used by all.

STEP ONE: What did I hear?

STEP TWO: I wonder what this story can mean?

STEP THREE: What can I say to Jesus for this great gift?

Conclusion

We are constantly observing and absorbing the world around us. We make judgments or draw conclusions about what we have observed. Then we respond to those judgments and conclusions by making choices in how to live.

When we follow this process of reflection on experience in light of the gospel, we nurture a Christian conscience and a way of seeing the world through the word of God. This becomes how God speaks to us today. It becomes as natural as breathing in and breathing out. In this way, we can see that God is directly involved in our lives, not disconnected from everyday experience. We come to see our personal experience in light of God's word so the God we come to experience is not "out there" but a personal, intimate God here with us in the reality of life.

And we begin to see that the stories of our lives are part of the unfolding larger story of God's unending love for us, generation after generation.

If we work at making this kind of reflection a habit, we soon will see that the Word of God applies to every aspect of our lives. Like our young friend in the opening story, we will become so filled with joy at that knowledge that we, too, will say, "I can't wait to tell!" And isn't that why you became a catechist?

1 When have I been surprised by an insight from sacred Scripture?

____

____

____

2 What are some ways I have come to see the story of my life as part of the larger story of God's unending love?

____

____

____

Try This

Create a plan for adapting one of the models of _Lectio divina_ presented in this chapter for one of your catechetical experiences.

ABOUT THE CONTRIBUTORS

General Editor

Sr. Angela Ann Zukowski, MHSH, DMin, is the Director of the Institute for Pastoral Initiatives (1978- present) and Professor in the Department of Religious Studies of the University of Dayton. She is a member of the Mission Helpers of the Sacred Heart (Towson, MD).

Chapter 1

Margaret Ralph, PhD, is the author of 15 books including the bestseller *And God Said What? An Introduction to Biblical Literary Forms* (Mahwah, NJ: Paulist Press, 2003), and the three-cycle series *Breaking Open the Lectionary* (Mahwah, NJ: Paulist Press, 2007), and *Scripture Basics: A Catechist's Guide* (New London, CT: Twenty-Third Publications, 2016).

Chapter 2

Most Reverend Anthony G. Bosco was the bishop of the Diocese of Greensburg, PA, until his death in 2013. He had a long history of involvement in Catholic radio and television and was recognized for his outstanding pastoral and compassionate ministry within his diocese.

Chapter 3

Sr. Angela Ann Zukowski, MHSH, DMin (See General Editor above.)

Chapter 4

William P. Roberts, PhD, professor of theology at the University of Dayton, is the author/editor of fifteen books, including *Marriage, It's a God Thing* (Cincinnati: St. Anthony Messenger, 2007).

Chapter 5

Sue Grenough, EdD, has worked extensively in the field of catechesis as a parish and a diocesan director of religious education. She teaches religious studies at Spalding University in Louisville, KY, and frequently gives retreats and workshops.

Chapter 6

Fr. Bertrand Buby, SM, STD, is a professor at the International Marian Research Institute at the University of Dayton in Dayton, OH. He has taught Scripture for over forty years and has specialized in Marian topics. Fr. Buby has published five books on Mary.

Chapter 7

Joyce M. Kelleher, MA, before her retirement, was the Secretary for Catechetical Services in the Diocese of Cleveland. Mrs. Kelleher taught in both public and Catholic high schools and colleges and has been a catechist, parish DRE, diocesan director, and seminary instructor.

RECOMMENDED RESOURCES

The following are available from the United States Conference of Catholic Bishops or your local Catholic bookstore

National Directory for Catechesis. Washington, DC: United States Conference of Catholic Bishops, 2005

General Directory for Catechesis. Washington, DC. Congregation for the Clergy. United States Conference of Catholic Bishops, 1997

New American Bible, Revised Edition. United States Conference of Catholic Bishops, 2011

Catechism of the Catholic Church. Vatican City. Second Edition. 1997

Available online at www.vatican.va

Dogmatic Constitution on Divine Revelation (Dei Verbum). Second Vatican Council, 1965

The Word of God in the Life and Mission of the Church (Instrumentum Laboris). Synod of Bishops, 2008

Dogmatic Constitution on the Church (Lumen Gentium). Second Vatican Council, 1964

Paths of the Church (Ecclesiam Suam). Second Vatican Council, 1964

Declaration on the Relation of the Church to Non-Christian Religions (Nostra Aetate). Second Vatican Council, 1965

Decree on Ecumenism (Unitatis Redintegratio). Second Vatican Council, 1964